Copyright © 2020 by Marcella Morse
Published by Marcella Morse

GOD'S CREATURES

GOD'S CREATURES

written and Illustrated   by   Marcella Morse

God made creatures to make the world a beautiful place.

From the smallest insect like the Fairyflies.

To the biggest animal the Blue Whale.

To the great feelings we have.

And the love we give, God had a purpose.

God wanted all animals and humans to have the same love for another.

He made animals to see inside your soul.

He made animals to make humans happy.

He made animals to bring down stress levels but most of all God made animals forgiving creatures.

For humans God wanted them to be a lot like animals in many ways like having instincts from the birds building there nest for their homes.

To the ducks protecting their ducklings we all have the same instincts.

The same way with cows that give their calves milk we all have the lovable bond with your loved ones.

But somehow animals are different, like they know when crisis is going to happen in the environment.

Although humans have gifted skills that animals don't, like being a scientist or a veterinarian but somehow God made us like this.

God had a purpose for everyone on this earth from sea creatures

to wildlife

And even you so let us combine the love with each other to make the world a beautiful place.

Dedicated to all the creatures that are suffering in this world.

Books you may like published by Marcella Morse

If you what to see more about author go to

Fine Art America
YouTube
Facebook-Marcella Morse Art
Instagram

About the author

Marcella Morse is from California. Her favorite things are hiking, enjoying nature, painting, and most of all animals. When she was a child she loved to draw portraits of family members and cats she grew up with. In school Marcella was fascinated with the arts so she tried computer graphic classes but in the end she was leaning toward painting and now she combines everything she loves to show people her passion.

www.ingramcontent.com/pod-product-compliance
Lightning Source LLC
Chambersburg PA
CBRC091505220426
43669CB00005B/42